edited by Julie Johnson

designer
denim™

GARDEN INSPIRATION
page 4

MINISKIRT, MAXI TOTE
page 8

Table of Contents

E-mail: Customer_Service@DRGnetwork.com

Designer Denim is published by DRG, 306 East Parr Road, Berne, IN 46711, telephone (260) 589-4000. Printed in USA. Copyright © 2008 DRG. All rights reserved. This publication may not be reproduced in part or in whole without written permission from the publisher.

HOUSE of WHITE BIRCHES PUBLISHERS SINCE 1947

RETAIL STORES: If you would like to carry this pattern book or any other DRG publications, call the Wholesale Department at Annie's Attic to set up a direct account: (903) 636-4303. Also, request a complete listing of publications available from DRG.

Every effort has been made to ensure that the instructions in this pattern book are complete and accurate. We cannot, however, take responsibility for human error, typographical mistakes or variations in individual work.

ISBN: 978-1-59217-223-8
1 2 3 4 5 6 7 8 9

STAFF
Editor: Julie Johnson
Managing Editor: Dianne Schmidt
Technical Artist: Nicole Gage
Technical Editor: Marla Freeman
Copy Supervisor: Michelle Beck
Copy Editors: Mary O'Donnell, Renée Wright

Graphic Arts Supervisor: Ronda Bechinski
Graphic Artists: Erin Augsburger, Joanne Gonzalez
Art Director: Brad Snow
Assistant Art Director: Nick Pierce
Photography Supervisor: Tammy Christian
Photography: Matthew Owen
Photo Stylist: Tammy Steiner

We've Got You Covered

Denim has a long history and a rather checkered past. The word denim came from a French material: *serge de Nîmes*. Serge is a durable twill-weave cloth made of a wool/silk blend. It was produced in Nîmes, a town in France. De Nîmes can be traced to the 16th century and came to England by the end of the 17th.

Its history started as a cloth known for its durability and strength, which was worn by workers and laborers. Often dyed with indigo, a dye found in the Americas, the fiber content changed to a cotton duck cloth. With the addition of copper rivets added by Levi Strauss' partner, Jacob Davis, who made riveted clothing for miners in 1872, its form became similar to the denim we find today.

Fast-forward to the 1940s, when denim became the preferred off-duty dress for soldiers who wore their Levi's while stationed overseas. By the 1950s, bad boys Marlon Brando and James Dean wore denim as a symbol of teenage rebellion, causing its popularity to flourish with American teens.

During the 1960s and '70s, denim was embroidered, painted, appliquéd and adorned with metal studs. Worn raggy and low, it grew bells on flared legs. In non-Western cultures, it become a symbol of Western decadence.

By the 1980s, denim became high-fashion as designers—Calvin Klein, Gloria Vanderbilt and Armani—labeled brands.

With the addition of Lycra in the 1990s, denim styles changed once again. Lycra added comfort and fit to our less-than-perfect aging bodies.

Today denim is back, even better than before. That's why you have this pattern book. Take your denim design up a notch by creating your own unique style. Whether you want to dress it up, cut it out, embellish it or transform it into something else, you'll love being the designer of denim.

Yes, we've got you covered.

Julie

Julie Johnson, editor

DRESS-UP JEANS
page 14

Garden Inspiration

DESIGN BY CHRIS MALONE

Grow your own garden by appliquéing fat-quarter flowers and vines onto a stylish vest.

FINISHED SIZE
Your size

MATERIALS
- Denim vest with collar
- Fabric:
    - fat quarter green mini dot for vines
    - fat quarter blue print for ruched trim
    - 1 (4½ x 8-inch) rectangle each 2 red prints for flower corsage
    - scraps 6 green prints for leaves
    - scraps 6 yellow/gold prints for small flowers
- Thin fleece or batting
- Scrap red felt
- 8 x 4½ inches paper-backed fusible adhesive
- Buttons:
    - ⅞-inch shank (any color)
    - 6 (½-inch) yellow
- ¾-inch pin back
- Permanent fabric adhesive
- Basic sewing supplies and equipment

INSTRUCTIONS

1. Cut a 1 x 22-inch bias strip from green mini dot fat quarter. Fold in half lengthwise, wrong sides together, and sew ¼ inch from long raw edge. Trim seam to a scant ⅛ inch. Refold, centering stitched seam on the back. Press. Repeat with a 1 x 15-inch strip of green mini dot fabric.

2. Referring to photo for placement, position green mini dot bias strips seam side down on vest, beginning with longer strip on right front,

curving over the shoulder and across the back yoke. Trim excess and pin in place. Start the shorter strip near the end of the first and drape it over the left shoulder to the front. Trim excess and pin in place. Hand-stitch in place.

3. Using template provided (page 7), prepare 10 vine leaves for turned-edge appliqué using your preferred method. Make two from each of the five green fabrics and reverse the pattern for half of the leaves. Position the leaves along the vine and hand-stitch in place.

4. Apply fusible web to wrong side of one red print rectangle. Remove paper backing and fuse the wrong side of the second red print rectangle to the first. From this bonded piece, cut two 3½ x 4½-inch rectangles.

HOUSE OF WHITE BIRCHES, BERNE, INDIANA 46711　DRGNETWORK.COM

5. Fold one rectangle in half to measure 1¾ x 4½ inches. Hand-sew gathering stitches ⅜ inch from the raw edges. Beginning ⅛ inch from one short end, cut into the fold at ⅛-inch intervals clear across the rectangle, ending each cut ⅛ inch from stitches (Figure 1). Pull thread to gather tightly. Stitch to connect the ends to form the flower. Repeat with the second rectangle, folding so the contrasting side faces out. Place one flower on top of the other and glue together at the center.

Figure 1

6. To make the flower center, glue a layer of fleece to the top of the shank button; cut away excess fleece. Cut a 1¾-inch circle from one of the red prints to contrast with the top flower. Sew a gathering stitch around the edge of the fabric circle, place the button, fleece side down, inside the circle and pull the thread to gather the fabric over the button. Knot and clip the thread. Glue the button to the flower with the shank inside the flower center hole. Cut a 1-inch circle from the felt scrap and sew the pin back to one

side. Glue the felt to the back of the flower. Pin the corsage to the top of the right front pocket.

7. Use the template to trace five small flower petals onto the wrong side of each of the six yellow/gold fabrics. Fold the fabric in half, right sides together, with the pattern on top. Pin to a piece of fleece. Sew on traced line, leaving the bottom edge open. Cut out, leaving a ⅛-inch seam allowance; clip curves. Apply seam sealant to bottom edges and let dry. Turn each petal right side out and press. Quilt around each petal using matching thread.

8. To form a flower, use doubled thread to make small gathering stitches along the bottom of a petal. Pick up another petal from the same fabric and gather along the bottom. Continue until all five petals are attached. Pull thread to gather tightly and knot. Take a small stitch into the first petal to finish the flower. Knot and clip the thread. Repeat to make a total of six flowers.

9. Use template to trace four small leaves on the wrong side of green fabric. Make padded appliqués in same manner as in step 7, except sew all around edges. After cutting out, make a slash through one layer of fabric only and turn right side out through the slash. Press. Hand-sew down the center of each leaf with green thread and a small running stitch.

10. Sew a yellow button to the center of each flower, attaching each flower to the vest as shown in photo. Tack one leaf to the top and bottom of the vertical row of flowers. Tack two leaves to one side of the horizontal row of flowers.

11. To make ruched trim for the collar, measure the distance from the inside corner of the collar around to the opposite corner. Multiply this measurement by 2.5 for the approximate length of trim needed. From blue print fat quarter, cut 1½-inch-wide bias strips to produce this length when joined. Join strips with diagonal seams; trim to ¼ inch and press open.

12. Press a ¼-inch hem at each short end of the strip. Fold under ¼ inch along one long raw edge and press. Fold opposite long raw edge almost to the bottom of the hem and press (Figure 2).

Figure 2

13. On the long folded edge, beginning ½ inch from one end of the strip, mark dots 1 inch apart across the top edge. On the opposite edge, begin 1 inch from the end to mark dots 1 inch apart (Figure 3). Using doubled matching thread, hand-sew a running stitch from the first dot at the top edge to the first dot at the bottom edge, then continue sewing in a zigzag pattern, gathering as you sew and ending at the last dot on the top edge. Measure trim and adjust gathers to match the measurement taken in step 11. Leave thread loose for further adjustments.

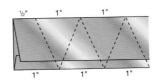

Figure 3

14. Beginning at inside corner of collar, tack ruched trim to edge, concealing stitches in folds of trim. At opposite end, knot gathering stitches and tack end into place. ❖

Sources: HeatnBond Lite fusible adhesive from Therm O Web; Fabri-Tac permanent fabric adhesive from Beacon Adhesives Inc.

TIPS & TECHNIQUES

Try using permanent fabric adhesive to attach the collar trim, and small flowers and leaves. The vine leaves can be attached with fusible adhesive. Remove the corsage for washing and for pinning on other clothing.

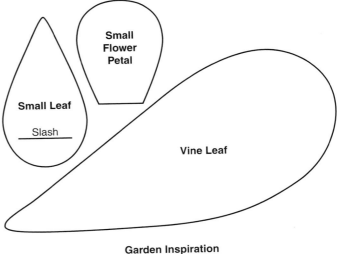

Small Leaf

Slash

Small Flower Petal

Vine Leaf

Garden Inspiration
Templates
Actual Size

Miniskirt, Maxi Tote

DESIGN BY CHRIS MALONE

Turn last year's miniskirt into this year's maxi tote
by following the simple steps in this design.

FINISHED SIZE
Size will vary

MATERIALS
- Denim miniskirt
- ¾ yard 44/45-inch-wide rust-print fabric for lining
- Scrap fabric for appliqués:
    - 3 gold/rust prints
    - 2 blue prints
    - 3 green prints
- ⅛ yard thin batting or fleece
- Man's silk tie in coordinating color
- Dark green size 5 pearl cotton
- Embroidery needle
- Basic sewing supplies and equipment

PROJECT NOTE
Finished size is determined by size of skirt. Model project used a size 11 denim skirt and measures approximately 20 x 16 inches, excluding handle.

INSTRUCTIONS
1. Cut off skirt hem. Place a sheet of pattern-tracing paper on work surface and smooth out the skirt on the paper with the front side up, snapped and zipped, and side seams even. Draw around the skirt, using the lower edge of the waistband as the top line and the cut edge as the bottom line. Add ½ inch seam allowance on all sides.

2. From rust-print fabric, use paper pattern to cut two lining pieces; also cut two 8½ x 5-inch rectangles for the lining pocket.

3. Trace template (page 11) for large flower onto wrong sides of gold/rust fabric scraps. Fold fabric in half with right sides together and pattern on top. Pin to fleece. Sew on traced lines and cut out ⅛ inch from stitching. Slash through 1 layer only of fabric. Clip curves and turn right side out through slash. Repeat to make a total number of padded appliqués as follows:
- one large gold/rust flower with gold/rust center.
- one large gold/rust flower with blue center.
- one blue medium flower with gold/rust center.
- one blue medium flower with blue center.
- one gold/rust medium flower with blue center.
- one gold/rust small flower with gold/rust center.
- eight leaves from three green prints.

4. Draw a curved vein line on each leaf and embroider a running stitch (see illustration) on the line using pearl cotton. Stitch centers to flowers. Arrange five flowers and six leaves on skirt front, and one medium flower and two leaves on the back pocket. Sew in place. ***Note:*** *Take care not to stitch into front pocket linings or through back pocket into skirt.*

Running Stitch

5. Cut the tip from the narrow end of the tie. Measuring from the cut end, cut a 27-inch

length. Measuring from the tip of the wide end, cut a 13-inch length. Cut a 4-inch length from the remainder of the tie. Sew ends of 27-inch length inside skirt waistband at each side with right side of tie facing out. Machine-stitch in place along stitching on waistband (Figure 1). Set remaining tie sections aside.

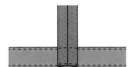

Figure 1

6. Sew lining pocket pieces right sides together using a ¼-inch seam and leaving an opening on one side for turning. Clip corners and turn right side out. Fold in seam allowance on opening and press. Pin pocket to right side of one lining piece centered and 2½ inches from top edge. Sew pocket around side and bottom edges. Sew a straight line down center of pocket to divide it (Figure 2).

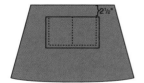

Figure 2

7. With right sides together, using a ½-inch seam allowance, sew lining on side and bottom edges. Press seams open. Press a ½-inch hem along top edge. Fold bottom seam to match side seams. Measure 1 inch from the tip and draw a 2-inch perpendicular line across the bottom. Sew on this line to box the bottom (Figure 3). Trim seam allowance to ¼ inch.

Figure 3

8. Turn skirt inside out. Sew bottom seam using a ½-inch seam allowance. Box in same manner as for lining (Step 7). Turn right side out. Insert lining in bag, matching side seams. Slipstitch hemmed edge of lining to bottom edge of waistband.

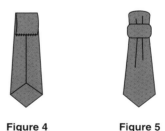

Figure 4   **Figure 5**

9. Fold under cut edge of 13-inch length of tie ½ inch, then fold 2½ inches to the back. Slipstitch in place (Figure 4). Wrap the 4-inch length of tie around it 1½ inches from the fold, pleating the tie, tacking ends at the back to secure (Figure 5). Hand-stitch tie embellishment to waistband at the side. ❖

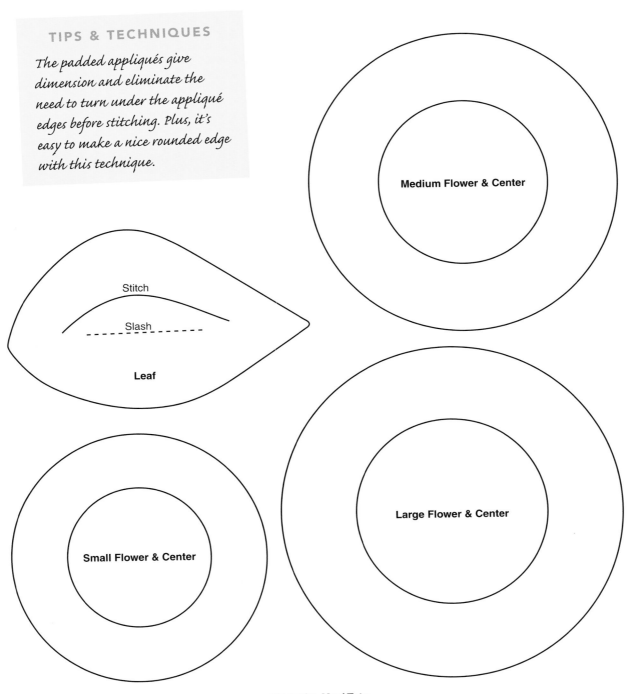

TIPS & TECHNIQUES

The padded appliqués give dimension and eliminate the need to turn under the appliqué edges before stitching. Plus, it's easy to make a nice rounded edge with this technique.

Medium Flower & Center

Stitch

Slash

Leaf

Small Flower & Center

Large Flower & Center

Miniskirt, Maxi Tote
Padded Flower & Leaf Templates
Actual Size

Suede Placket Jacket

DESIGN BY CAROL ZENTGRAF

It's easy to transform a denim jacket from basic to "wow" when you cover the placket, collar and cuffs with faux suede fabric.

FINISHED SIZE
Your size

MATERIALS
- Denim jacket with mandarin collar
- ½ yard faux suede fabric
- Self-adhesive double-sided basting tape
- Teflon or walking foot
- Basic sewing supplies and equipment

INSTRUCTIONS

1. Remove buttons from jacket and mark their placement. **Note:** *For riveted buttons, see step 2.*

2. Trace plackets, collar and cuffs onto tracing paper and cut out patterns. Mark placement of buttonholes and buttons on pattern pieces. Use the patterns to cut two right and two left plackets, two collars (reverse one) and two cuffs, cutting the fabric ⅛ inch beyond the edges of the patterns. If placing placket or cuffs over riveted buttons, mark and cut out buttonholes at button placement on these pieces to slide over riveted buttons.

3. On the wrong side of each suede piece, apply a strip of basting tape along each long edge. Remove backing from the tape and center the suede plackets on each side of the jacket front plackets. Using Teflon or walking foot, stitch the layers together ⅛ inch from the edges of the suede plackets. Cut out buttonholes on buttonhole placket.

4. Repeat to apply suede collar and cuffs. **Note:** *Suede cuffs are sewn to outside of jacket only.*

5. Resew buttons to jacket sewing through denim and suede layers. To tightly secure buttons, position a clear button behind each outside button. ❖

Source: Wonder basting tape from Prym Consumer USA Inc.

Dress-Up Jeans

DESIGN BY CAROL ZENTGRAF

Getting a designer look for less is so simple when you embellish your jeans with embroidery and paint. Use an open embroidery design and fill in the open spaces for a one-of-a-kind look.

FINISHED SIZE
Your size

MATERIALS
- Denim jeans with flared legs and plain leg seams
- 4½ x 4½-inch outline machine-embroidery design
- Tear-away stabilizer
- Fabric paint in coordinating color and small paintbrush
- Rayon machine-embroidery thread in coordinating color
- Embroidery machine
- Basic sewing supplies and equipment

PROJECT NOTE
If your sewing machine doesn't have embroidery capabilities, you can adapt this design by drawing or copying an open motif onto tear-away stabilizer. Open pant leg as in step 1. Use temporary spray adhesive to adhere stabilizer to the pant leg and stitch. Remove stabilizer and follow steps 5 and 6.

INSTRUCTIONS
1. Remove stitching from inner leg seams. Open legs flat.

2. If available, use embroidery-machine software to group two motifs vertically. With stabilizer on the wrong side of the fabric area, hoop the center of one leg so the embroidered design will be approximately 3 inches above the hem and centered on the outer leg seam.

3. Embroider the grouped design, or embroider two designs vertically. Remove the hoop and tear-away excess stabilizer. Vertically flip the design and embroider two more designs 3 inches above the two lower designs, again centered on the outer leg seam. Tear away excess stabilizer and trim jump threads.

4. Repeat steps 2 and 3 for opposite leg.

5. Using a small amount of paint, paint between embroidered lines to fill in areas as desired. Let dry and heat-set following manufacturer's instructions.

6. Sew inner leg seams closed. ❖

Sources: SoSoft fabric paint from DecoArt; Tear-Easy stabilizer from Sulky of America.

Suede-Accent Skirt

DESIGN BY CAROL ZENTGRAF

Give a basic denim skirt with a front slit a designer look when you embellish it with faux suede.

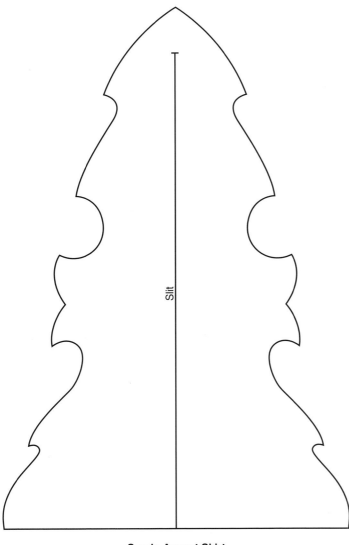

Suede-Accent Skirt
Skirt Front Panel Template
Enlarge 200%

FINISHED SIZE
Your size

MATERIALS
- Denim skirt
- 8 x 12 inches faux suede fabric
- 8 x 12-inch sheet double-stick fusible web
- Teflon or walking foot
- Basic sewing supplies and equipment

PROJECT NOTE
This project is easier to do with a skirt that has a center front seam. If your skirt does not have a center front seam, follow the directions below, but after you cut the center front to the desired length, edge-finish raw edges before adding the faux suede.

INSTRUCTIONS
1. Enlarge the skirt front panel template as indicated. ***Note:*** *Adjust height of template as needed to fit the slit in skirt.*

2. Trace template onto the paper side of fusible web. Cut out just outside traced line. Apply to wrong side of suede fabric. Cut out on traced line.

3. Measure the desired center front opening on the skirt along the front seam. Mark. Carefully cut open the stitches from the bottom edge to the mark. Cut a matching slit this length in the center of the suede, cutting from the straight bottom edge up.

HOUSE OF WHITE BIRCHES, BERNE, INDIANA 46711   DRGNETWORK.COM

4. Press cut seam edges to the inside of the skirt. Pin and baste into place.

5. Remove paper backing and adhere suede to the front of the skirt, aligning the bottom and opening edges. Use a press cloth to fuse in place.

6. Edgestitch using a Teflon or walking foot. ❖

Source: *Steam-A-Seam2 double-stick fusible web from The Warm Company.*

Kitschy Clutch

DESIGN BY SHEILA ZENT

Casual meets kitsch with this petite purse that pairs denim with bold rhinestones. Play up color by matching the zipper with rhinestones and blue-jean topstitching.

FINISHED SIZE
10 x 5½ x 1¾ inches

MATERIALS
- ¼ yard 44/45-inch-wide denim fabric or recycled blue jeans to fit patterns
- ¼ yard 44/45-inch-wide lime-green lining fabric
- Craft-weight fusible interfacing
- 6 x 12-inch piece quilt batting
- 9-inch lime green nylon zipper
- 18mm glue-on rhinestones:
     13 blue
     14 lime green
- Rhinestone glue
- Thread:
     denim blue for construction
     lime green for topstitching
- Optional: 1½ inches ¾-inch-wide black hook-and-loop tape for pocket closure
- Basic sewing supplies and equipment

INSTRUCTIONS
Note: *Use a ½-inch seam allowance unless otherwise stated.*

1. Copy clutch front/back and pocket patterns (page 20), enlarging 200 percent to make full-size patterns. Placing clutch front/back pattern on fold, cut two from denim, two from interfacing and two from lining. Placing pocket pattern on fold, cut one from denim, one from batting and one from lining. Also cut one 2 x 13-inch long strip from denim for wrist strap.

2. Fuse interfacing to wrong sides of clutch front and back. Transfer • marks to the right side of each piece. At the top edge of each piece, press under ¼ inch. Pin clutch front along one side of zipper tape with folded edge to the outside of the zipper teeth and topstitch in place. Repeat with clutch back on opposite side of zipper (Figure 1).

Figure 1

3. Baste denim pocket and batting pocket pieces together around outer edges. With right sides together, stitch pocket lining to layered denim pocket along top edge. Fold lining to back and press edge. Pin pocket layers together around side and bottom edges and baste. Transfer topstitching lines to pocket front and topstitch.

4. Place pocket on clutch front, matching bottom edges and corners. Baste layers together close to raw edges. **Optional:** *Apply hook-and-loop tape closure to pocket and front before basting.*

HOUSE OF WHITE BIRCHES, BERNE, INDIANA 46711   DRGNETWORK.COM

5. Press strip for wrist strap in half lengthwise with wrong sides together. Unfold and press both raw edges into the fold. Press in half again. Topstitch close to each long edge (Figure 2). Fold strap in half to make a loop and baste the short raw ends together.

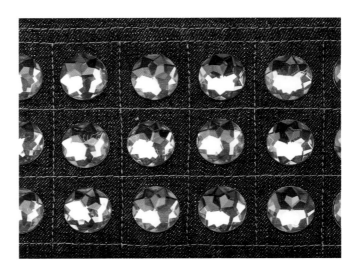

Figure 2

6. With right sides together, stitch clutch front to back along side and bottom edges, leaving cut-out corners open. Press seam allowances open. Reposition bottom corners to match side and bottom seams and pin. Stitch to create a box shape (Figure 3).

7. Slit top corners to the • marks. Box top corners in same manner as bottom corners, inserting the strap end at the top of the zipper.

8. Assemble clutch lining in same manner as clutch. Press under ¼ inch on top edge. Place lining in clutch and hand-stitch around zipper opening.

9. Remove transfer markings according to manufacturer's directions. Glue rhinestones to front of bag as shown in photo. ❖

Figure 3

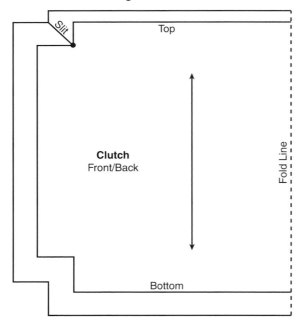

Clutch
Front/Back

Slit

Top

Bottom

Fold Line

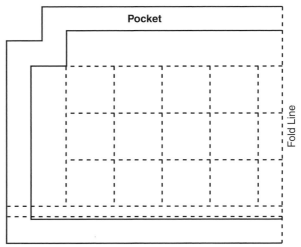

Pocket

Fold Line

Kitschy Clutch
Templates
Enlarge 200%

A Jeans Affair

DESIGNS BY DIANE BUNKER

Jazz up your jeans and jacket with interesting appliqués cut from home decor fabrics and lace. Add a bit of sparkle with crystals, and you're ready for anything.

FINISHED SIZE
Your size

MATERIALS
- Denim jeans and jeans jacket
- 54–60-inch-wide home decor lace:
    - 1 yard ecru lace with a design motif
    - ½ yard ecru lace for jacket front yoke and pockets
- Assorted large scraps floral and solid-color jacquard-style tone-on-tone home-decor fabrics
- Paper-backed fusible web
- Clear monofilament thread
- Gold metallic embroidery thread
- Optional: burnt sienna Shiva Artist's Paintstik and ½-inch crescent paintbrush
- Optional: Sharp tool
- 3mm and 4mm heat-set crystals and heat-set applicator tool
- Basic sewing tools and equipment

INSTRUCTIONS
1. Remove the jeans back pockets. Test the shape and fit of the pocket templates (page 28) on the back pockets of your jeans. Cut two templates from the ecru lace and from fusible web.

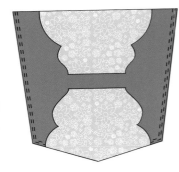

Figure 1

Fuse to the wrong side of lace. Remove paper backing and fuse to pockets (Figure 1).

2. Cut two 3½-inch squares from one floral fabric. Apply fusible web, position on back pockets and fuse. Straight-stitch 1⁄16 inch around the raw edges of each piece and satin-stitch.

6. Plan the floral and design motif lace appliqué design for each yoke. Apply fusible web, arrange and fuse to yoke. Straight-stitch ¹⁄₁₆ inch around the raw edges of each piece and satin-stitch. Hand-tack lace slits around buttons as needed.

7. Design and apply appliqués to the jacket back referring to steps 4, 5 and 6.

8. Apply crystals randomly using heat-set tool following manufacturer's instructions. Turn garment inside out to launder. ❖

Source: Swarovski hot-fix crystals and BeJeweler hot-fix applicator tool from Creative Crystals Co.

3. Using the photo as a guide, cut the desired shapes for legs from design motif lace, floral and tone-on-tone fabrics. Apply fusible web, position as desired and fuse. Working from the bottom layer, straight-stitch ¹⁄₁₆ inch around the raw edges of each piece and satin-stitch.

Optional: *To "antique" the lace, dry-brush it with a burnt sienna Paintstik then heat-set with your iron following the manufacturer's directions.*

4. Use tracing paper to trace the front jacket yoke. Add ½-inch seam allowances and cut out the yoke front pattern. Cut two jacket front yokes from ecru lace, reversing one.

5. Position lace yokes, right sides up on each yoke, and sew in place (Figure 2). Repeat stitching ⅛ inch inside the first stitching. Trim excess lace. **Note:** *If the piece must go over a button, cut a small slit to slip lace around button. Excess lace will extend past yoke finished edges.*

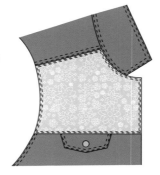

Figure 2

No-Sweat Denim

DESIGN BY JULIE JOHNSON

Use the legs from an old pair of jeans to transform a sweatshirt into a causal jacket.

FINISHED SIZE
Your size

MATERIALS
- Demin jeans
- Sweatshirt in your size
- Fat quarter coordinating fabric
- ⅛ yard 60-inch-wide fusible tricot interfacing
- 2 no-sew snaps
- 2 sets hook-and-eye closures
- Water-soluble thread
- Water-soluble tape
- Fusible tape
- Assorted coordinating buttons
- Basic sewing supplies and equipment

SWEATSHIRT PREPARATION

1. Prewash and dry the sweatshirt. Determine the center front of the sweatshirt by placing wrong sides together and matching shoulder seams at neck intersection. Pin side seams from the bottom rib to the beginning of the armscye. Lay the sweatshirt flat; lightly pat toward center front (Figure 1). Mark center front at neck and lower rib edges.

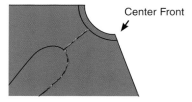

Figure 1

2. Turn the sweatshirt to the wrong side. Slide a narrow mat between the sweatshirt front and back. Use a long ruler to connect markings and mark with marking pen or chalk. Prior to cutting, stabilize each side of the center front with water-soluble tape positioned ¼ inch from the center-line (Figure 2). Use a long ruler and rotary cutter to open center front. Turn sweatshirt to right side.

Figure 2

3. Set sewing machine to a narrow zigzag. Staystitch ⅛ inch from the ribbing on the sweatshirt fabric with water-soluble thread to stabilize the neck, cuff and waist edges before removing ribbing. Trim ribbing using a 5-inch embroidery scissors by clipping between staystitching and ribbing (Figure 2).

ASSEMBLY

Note: *Use ¼-inch seam allowance throughout.*

1. Face the back of the sweatshirt by placing the sweatshirt flat with the front open. Place paper behind the back neck and draw the back neck curve. Trim. Place paper pattern on top of the inside shirt back. Measure about 5 inches down the center back and draw a semicircular shape to the shoulder seam, leaving a 1-inch width from the neck point (Figure 3). Shape shoulder

seams. Use paper template to cut facing from denim. Fuse tricot interfacing to the wrong side of denim.

Figure 3

2. From fat quarter of coordinating fabric cut 35 inches total of 1½-inch-wide strips on the bias. Sew the strips together by placing wrong sides together to make an L and sew diagonally (Figure 4). Trim and finger-press seam to one side. Fold in half lengthwise with wrong sides together; press. Fold raw edges to meet at center fold and press to make bias tape. **Note:** *Try using the Clover Bias Tape Maker to make bias tape.*

Figure 4

3. Place bias tape on wrong side of back facing, matching raw edges. Stitch into place. Fold tape over back facing. Fold raw edge under and sew in place. Lightly apply temporary spray adhesive to the wrong side of the facing and position along the neck seam. Topstitch back facing into place.

4. Cut a 1 x 5-inch piece of denim for back loop. Sew by folding in half with wrong sides together and turning raw edges under. Press. Topstitch on each side. Fold back loop in half, and position in the center back of sweatshirt; press (Figure 5). Stitch into place.

Figure 5

5. Measure the length around the bottom of the sweatshirt; divide by two and add ½ inch. Cut two 3-inch-wide strips of denim this length for hem strips. With right sides facing, sew the two hem strips of denim together along one short side. Press seam open. Fold hem strip in half, wrong sides together, matching long edges. Press. Open fold to apply fusible tape on the wrong side of one long edge of the hem strip. Using your serger or sewing machine, edge-finish the edge of the hem strip over the tape.

6. With right sides together and raw edges even, serge or stitch the unfinished edge of the hem strip to the lower edge of the sweatshirt. Lightly press seam toward the hem strip. Refold hem strip and press finished edge into place on the wrong side of the sweatshirt. Trim center front edges even. Topstitch top edge of hem strip.

7. Measure the length of the center front opening and add 2 inches. From denim, cut two 3-inch-wide strips this length for center front facings. On the wrong side of each front facing, apply fusible tape on one edge; edge-finish as before. Turn lower edge of front facing under ¼ inch. Match turned edge of front facing to lower edge of hem facing with right sides together and serge or stitch the unfinished edge of the front facing to the center front of the sweatshirt. Trim upper edge of front facing to match sweatshirt neck edge. Lightly press seam toward the front facing. Fold facing to wrong side and press into place. Double-topstitch center and serged edge.

8. Measure the neck edge and add ½ inch. Cut a 2½-inch-wide strip from denim this length for neck binding. Press one long edge of binding under ¼ inch. Press the other edge under ½ inch.

Figure 7

opening, measure 1 inch from the sleeve seam on the back side of the sweatshirt sleeve. Using the knit stitches in the sleeve as a guide, draw a straight line 3 inches long on the sleeve with a marking pen (Figure 7). **Note:** *The straight line will not run parallel to the sleeve seam.* Cut open.

11. Fold sleeve placket binding in half with wrong sides together. Turn raw edges under to center fold. Position right side of placket binding against the wrong side of the placket opening. Pin together with the center of the placket opening barely catching on the binding (Figure 8). Sew a scant ¼-inch seam, angling seam toward the center of the placket opening (Figure 9).

Figure 8

Figure 9

12. Fold placket binding to right side of placket opening catching the raw edges of the placket in the fold. Topstitch into place. Crease center placket binding and sew diagonally on the binding fold.

13. Measure the length of the cuff opening and add ½ inch. Cut two 5-inch-wide pieces of denim this length for cuffs. Fold each cuff in half with right sides together. Stitch short seams. Clip corners and turn cuff to right side. With raw edges even, place right side of one cuff layer against the wrong side of the sleeve, and sew cuff to sleeve. Lightly press seam into cuff.

14. Fold under remaining cuff raw edge. Pin folded edge of the cuff to the right side of sleeve. Topstitch into place. Continue topstitching around remaining three edges of each cuff.

Position the end of neck binding ¼ inch past the center front facing with the right side of the binding against the wrong side of the sweatshirt and the pressed ½-inch line along the raw edge of the neckline. Pin binding to the neckline, taking care to not distort the neckline and to cover the raw edges of the back loop. Extend the neck binding past the opposite center front by ¼ inch (Figure 6). Sew the binding to the neckline. Clip neckline as needed to lie flat. Lightly press neckline facing over the raw edges. **Note:** *You may need to steam neckline for shaping.* Fold neck binding to the right side of the sweatshirt.

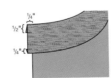

Figure 6

9. Turn under ¼-inch binding ends even with center fronts. Fold binding over raw edge to the front of the sweatshirt and topstitch along folded edge, taking care to catch the extended ends in the seam.

10. Cut two denim strips each 1½ x 8 inches for sleeve placket bindings. To make the placket

FINISHING

1. Mark placement of snaps on cuffs. Follow manufacturer's instructions for attaching.

2. Sew two hook-and-eye sets to neckline binding for front closure.

3. Arrange and sew buttons to front in a pleasing design. ❖

Sources: *Snaps from Snap Source, Wash-A-Way Wonder Tape, Wash-A-Way thread, Fray Block, Sullivan's Quilt Basting Spray, Clover Bias Tape Maker, Clover Pen-Style Chaco Liners, Water-Erasable Blue Marking Pen from Clotilde.com.*

A Jeans Affair

Continued from page 21

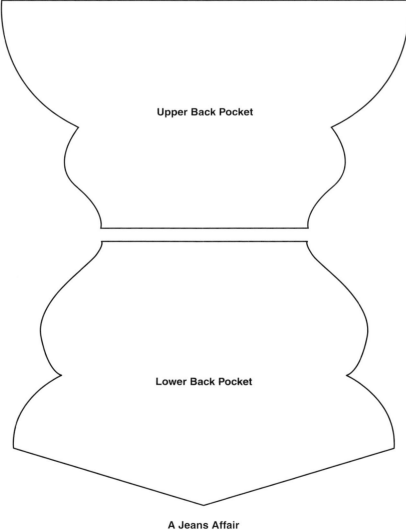

Upper Back Pocket

Lower Back Pocket

A Jeans Affair
Templates
Actual Size

A Step Back in Time

DESIGNS BY DIANE BUNKER

Use lace bits and trims to transform a ho-hum jean skirt into a work of art. It's so simple, you'll want to add designer flair to all your skirts.

FINISHED SIZE
Your size

MATERIALS
- 2 short straight denim skirts
- 6 x 11-inch rose-pattern stencil or stencil of choice
- 5¼ x 6¼-inch floral-pattern stencil or stencil of choice
- 2 oz white puff paint for each skirt
- Ultrafine iridescent glitter
- Clean empty file folder
- Painter's tape
- Temporary spray adhesive
- Flexible palette knife or old credit card
- Stencil-marking pad
- Soft paintbrush
- Sharpened wooden stick
- Freezer paper
- 7-inch white crocheted doily
- 15 inches white flat lace trim
- 18 (3mm) heat-set crystals
- Heat-set applicator tool
- Basic sewing supplies and equipment

PROJECT NOTES
Wash and dry skirt without fabric softener.

Iron freezer paper to the wrong side of the garment for stability.

Paint and spray adhesive build-up can be removed from the stencils using alcohol. Hand sanitizer can also be used to clean stencils and it's great for your hands.

Finished project is machine washable and dryable. Turn garment inside out and wash it separately for the first few washings. Dry with medium heat.

ROSE DENIM SKIRT
1. Fill container large enough to hold stencil with water and set nearby. Tape off the extra swirls and the leaf border on the stencil. Position stencil on one side of the skirt and mark the

placement with the stencil-marking pad following manufacturer's instructions. In well-ventilated area, spray the back of the stencil with adhesive. Blot off excess if needed. Reposition the stencil on the skirt.

2. Squeeze out a generous amount of white puff paint next to stencil openings at the top of the stencil. With palette knife or old credit card, begin pulling the puff paint across the stencil to cover all the cutouts. **Note:** *Use a light touch to avoid forcing the paint under the stencil.* Reapply paint as needed to cover the stencil. Carefully pull off the stencil and place it in container of water.

3. Quickly view the design for areas where puff paint may have seeped under. Use the sharpened stick to carefully wipe off excess and reshape as needed, or apply additional paint as needed with a soft brush. If beyond repair, paint may be quickly rinsed out with soap and water to start over **after** fabric has dried.

4. Add glitter while paint is wet, pouring on thick to cover the whole area. Let it set for an hour, then tap off excess into a file folder and back into the glitter bottle. Let dry completely.

5. Remove tape from swirls on stencil to position and apply to designs, referring to photo for placement. Apply swirls one at a time, doing the smaller swirls first. Let dry.

6. Repeat the entire process on the opposite side of the skirt, reversing the design. Let dry completely.

7. Shake skirt outside to remove excess glitter. Turn skirt inside out; remove freezer paper. Hover steam iron over the design area and steam to activate puff paint. Turn right side out.

8. Fold doily in half and mark the fold line. Sew a zigzag stitch across the doily ¼ inch on each side of marked line, then cut on marked line. Sew lace trim across raw edge of each doily half.

9. Fold each doily in half to find the center point. Pin the center of each doily to the sides of the skirt with lace-trimmed edges of doilies even with skirt hem. Sew edges of doilies to skirt using a zigzag stitch, then cut the skirt away leaving at least ½ inch of fabric. Clip curved edge and press under for a clean hem. Sew trim to each doily using a straight stitch.

10. Follow manufacturer's instructions to randomly apply crystals using heat-set applicator tool. Model project used nine crystals on each side of skirt.

FLORAL DENIM SKIRT

1. Fill container large enough to hold stencil with water and set nearby. Beginning at one side of skirt along bottom edge, position stencil and mark the placement with the stencil-marking pad following manufacturer's instructions. **Note:** *Stencil on model project was placed at an angle. Adjust the number of repeats depending on the size of the stencil and the skirt.* Mark stencil placement all around the bottom of the skirt. In well-ventilated area, spray the back of the stencil with adhesive. Blot off excess if needed. Reposition the stencil on the skirt.

2. Repeat Steps 2 and 3 of Rose Denim Skirt to apply paint to stencil patterns all around skirt. **Note:** *Allow one side of skirt to dry completely before applying paint to opposite side.* Let dry.

3. Turn skirt inside out; remove freezer paper. Hover steam iron over the design area and steam to activate puff paint. Turn right side out. ❖

Sources: *Rose With Swirls Stencil and Floral Stencil from Tiny Treasures From the Heart by Diane Bunker; puff paint from Jones Tones; Super 77 spray adhesive from 3M; Quilt Pounce stencil-marking pad from Hancy Mfg. Co.; heat-set crystals and BeJeweler Pro applicator tool from Creative Crystal Co.*

Ragtag Denim

DESIGN BY JULIE JOHNSON

Use your serger, fat quarters and denim to make a reversible tote.

FINISHED SIZE
14½ x 12 inches

MATERIALS
- Denim jeans
- 2 fat quarters coordinating fabric or 21 (5 x 5-inch) quilt-fabric charms
- ⅓ yard 60-inch-wide lightweight quilt batting
- Purse handles
- Serger*
- Basic sewing supplies and equipment

Assembled stacks may be zigzagged together and then straight-stitched to form the bag.

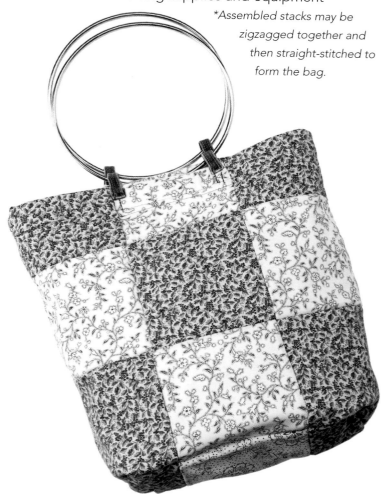

CUTTING

From jeans:
- Cut 21 (5 x 5-inch) squares.
- Cut four belt loops from jeans, or cut four 1 x 5-inch strips.

From one fat quarter:
- Cut 10 (5 x 5-inch) squares.

From second fat quarter:
- Cut 11 (5 x 5-inch) squares.

From batting:
- Cut 21 (4½ x 4½-inch) squares.

INSTRUCTIONS
Note: *Set serger to a wide 4-thread overlock.*

1. Arrange fat-quarter squares alternately, wrong sides up, in rows three squares wide by seven squares long.

2. Place a batting square in the center of each fat-quarter square. Top each with a denim square, right side up, to complete the stack.

3. Working row by row, serge stacks by placing right sides of fat quarters together.

Press serged seams in opposite directions by row. **Note:** *Use rotary cutter to trim rows even if needed.*

4. With right sides of fat quarters facing, butt pressed serged seams of rows together, and pin to secure. Serge, removing pins prior to stitching.

HOUSE OF WHITE BIRCHES, BERNE, INDIANA 46711   DRGNETWORK.COM

5. With fat-quarter sides together, fold bag in half matching seams on each side. Pin. Serge sides together removing pins prior to stitching. Straight-stitch close to serging to reinforce serged seam.

6. Box bag bottom by pulling the lower side seam corner and matching the serged seams together. Straight-stitch along serged side seams. Trim corner and straight-stitch to finish edge (Figure 1).

Figure 1

7. Serge bag top layers together. Fold fat-quarter side over denim by 1¾ inches. Pin, then double topstitch into place.

8. Using the middle 5-inch-square as a guide, straight-stitch or zigzag one belt loop end near the top edge of the bag. Slip loop over purse handle; sew the opposite end below the sewn loop on the opposite side of the bag. *Option: If using the 1 x 5 inch strips, fold strips in half lengthwise,* press and fold raw edges to center, making a ¼ x 5-inch strip. Turn raw edge under by ½ inch on each end. Attach as for belt loop.❖

Knit-Wit Denim

DESIGN BY PAULINE RICHARDS

Start with a sweater. Add some sturdy denim, and you'll be ready to make a one-of-a-kind comfy jacket.

FINISHED SIZE
Your size

MATERIALS
- 1½ yards 60-inch-wide denim*
- Blue pullover sweater (see Project Note)
- Maia jacket pattern by La Fred or princess-seamed jacket pattern of your choice
- 1¾ yards 25-inch-wide fusible interfacing
- 7 (¾-inch) buttons
- 2 (1 x 20-inch) strips tear-away stabilizer
- Basic sewing supplies and equipment

Amount may vary depending on size. Try using recycled thrift-store jeans instead of purchased denim.

PROJECT NOTE
When choosing a sweater, measure sleeve length from bottom of sleeve to the shoulder seam. The length should be as long as the sleeve pattern minus the hem allowance. Because many sweaters are designed with drop shoulders, the sleeves may be short. It may be necessary to select a sweater a size or two larger than normally worn to accommodate your sleeve length.

INSTRUCTIONS
1. Remove both sleeves from the sweater by cutting ⅜ inch past the sleeve seam into the body of the sweater. Set sleeves aside.

2. Fold sweater in half along the center back and match side seams. Place jacket side back pattern on sweater back. Place the finished lower ribbed sweater edge 1½ inches above the hem cutting line to match the 1½-inch hem allowance on the pattern. Cut out the jacket side back (Figure 1).

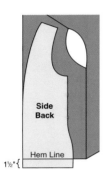

Figure 1

3. Fold sweater front in the same manner. Eliminate the pocket from the side jacket pattern piece and cut the jacket side fronts. Do not sew the front darts.

4. From denim, cut the jacket center back panel, the jacket fronts, front facings, back facing, upper collar and under collar. Cut and apply interfacing as directed on the pattern instruction sheet.

5. Fold sleeve pattern in half, matching underarm seam lines. Fold sleeves in half and place them over the folded pattern, matching the centers of the sleeves. Place sleeves over the pattern. Match the cuff edge to the hem fold line. Cut sleeves to fit.

Alternative: *If sleeves are smaller than the pattern it will be necessary to create a gusset extension pattern with seam allowances as shown in Figure 2. Cut gussets from knit fabric. Open sleeves from underarm down as far as necessary to accommodate the gusset (Figure 3), where point A is the point matching the side seam. The gusset widest width will meet with point A. Sew the gussets in place.*

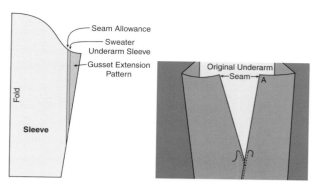

Figure 2   **Figure 3**

6. Construct garment according to pattern instructions. When joining knit fabric to woven fabric, sew with knit fabric against the feed dogs and woven fabric facing up. When joining knit fabric to knit fabric, cut 1-inch-wide strips of tear-away stabilizer the length of the finished seams. After pinning the knit layers together, pin the stabilizer strip in place, shaping the seam. Sew through all layers, then finish the seam and remove excess stabilizer. **Note:** *Some stabilizer will remain in the finished seam.* To eliminate bulk, press seams toward woven fabric and secure with topstitching (Figure 4). ❖

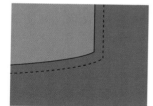

Figure 4

Source: *Jacket pattern from La Fred.*

Rosebud Vine

DESIGN BY DIANE BUNKER

You'll make a statement when you embellish your jeans with puff paint and crystals.

FINISHED SIZE
Your size

MATERIALS
- Denim jeans
- Mesh transfer canvas
- Black fine-point permanent marker
- Lightweight cardboard to fit inside legs and pocket
- 2 oz black puff paint
- Black fabric paint
- Resealable plastic bag
- Scotch brand Magic tape
- Black glitter
- Clean empty file folder
- 24 (3mm) heat-set crystals
- Heat-set applicator tool

PROJECT NOTES
Wash and dry jeans without fabric softener.

Place pieces of cardboard under the areas on which you will be working.

Puff paint is the consistency of softened butter, so it doesn't need much squeezing while you're painting the design. Practice on a paper towel to get the right flow.

The finished garment is machine washable and dryable. Turn garment inside out and wash separately for the first few washings. Dry with medium heat.

INSTRUCTIONS
1. Trace templates (page 39) onto mesh transfer canvas using a black fine-point permanent marker. ***Note:*** *Place a piece of tracing paper between the pattern and the cloth to protect the pattern.*

2. Pin the traced transfer canvas in place on the jeans. Retrace the lines with the marker to transfer the design through the canvas to the jeans. Repeat the pattern twice at the bottom of the right leg, adding the extra swirls at the top and bottom of the design. Reverse the template and trace once on the upper left leg. Trace the pocket template to one of the back pockets, then reverse template and trace onto the other pocket.

3. Squeeze the bottle of puff paint into a resealable plastic bag. Add approximately 20 percent of the black fabric paint to the bag to darken the puff paint. Close the bag and knead the two colors together. Cut one of the corners of the bag and squeeze the mixture back into the bottle. **Note:** *Not all will fit since you added extra paint.*

4. Wrap a piece of Magic tape at a slight angle to the top of the puff-paint applicator tip to form a smaller hole.

5. Insert cardboard inside legs and pockets. Beginning at the top, outline about 4 inches of the design. Carefully sprinkle on a black glitter, trying not to get it beyond what you have lined. Outline the next 4 inches and sprinkle with glitter. Continue to the bottom. Let dry one hour. Carefully shake off excess glitter into the file folder and pour back into its original container. Repeat for opposite leg.

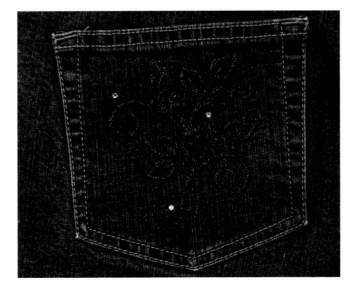

6. Let front dry four hours before turning over to do the back pockets. **Note:** *A hair dryer set at medium heat may be used to speed drying.* Add designs to back pockets in same manner and let dry completely.

7. Shake jeans outside to remove excess glitter. Turn jeans inside out. Hover steam iron over the design area and steam to activate puff paint. Turn the jeans right side out and reshake outside again.

8. Follow manufacturer's instructions to add crystals using heat-set applicator tool. Model projects used three on each pocket, 11 on the right leg, and seven on the left leg. ❖

Sources: *Puff paint from Jones Tones; heat-set crystals and BeJeweler Pro heat-set applicator tool from Creative Crystal Co.*

Bottom Leg

Top Leg

Middle Leg

Pockets

Rosebud Vine
Transfer Templates
Actual Size

Lady in Black

DESIGN BY LYNN WEGLARZ

Create a boutique look for your denim jacket
by inserting lace and adding trims.

FINISHED SIZE
Your size

MATERIALS
- Jean jacket*
- ½–⅝ yard 44/45-inch-wide embroidered black lace
- ½–⅝ yard 44/45-inch-wide black organza
- 1¼–1½ yards beaded lace trim
- Basic sewing supplies and equipment

Model project used jacket with back panel, yoke and waistband.

INSTRUCTIONS

1. Carefully unstitch back panel from jacket. Using back panel for pattern, cut one panel each from embroidered lace and organza.

2. Baste embroidered lace and organza panels together with organza panel on wrong side of lace panel.

3. With right sides together, pin and stitch sides of lace/organza panel to sides of jacket back-panel opening using ¼-inch seam allowance. Finish seams using serger or zigzag stitches. Topstitch seams following design of jacket.

4. Pin bottom edge of lace panel between layers of waistband. Baste. Topstitch seam following design of jacket.

5. Turn under top raw edges of lace panel and pin to bottom edge of jacket yoke. Baste. Topstitch seam following design of jacket.

6. Pin beaded lace trim along cuff edges, pocket edges and/or collar edges. Hand-stitch trim in place. ❖

Fun & Flouncy Skirt

DESIGN BY ZOE GRAUL

Make an old, tired pair of denim jeans or shorts into a fun flounced skirt. Save the scraps for a later project.

FINISHED SIZE
Your size

MATERIALS
- Denim jeans or shorts
- 60 x 60-inch-square semi-sheer silky fabric for underskirt
- 36- to 44-inch-square silk scarf for top skirt
- Two rubber bands for rose
- Basic sewing supplies and equipment

PROJECT NOTES
When cutting jeans, check to see where cutting line falls in relation to back pockets. If back pockets are below the cutting line, drop the line in the back to avoid cutting or sewing over the pockets. An uneven hemline is a good look for this project.

If front inside pockets are below the cutting line, they can be cut off and the pockets stitched closed after cutting the jeans.

TIPS & TECHNIQUES
This project is very versatile. The underskirt and top skirt could both be made from fabric circles in two different lengths. Or both layers could be made from scarves that are the same size, but with the points offset for a whimsical effect. The project also lends itself to a shorter skirt version for teens or the "young at heart."

INSTRUCTIONS
1. Lay jeans flat. Mark front cutting line by smoothing below the zipper to where the fabric starts to flare for the rise, approximately 1 inch below the zipper (Figure 1). Measure, and repeat for each side and back. Mark cutting line around jeans and cut off.

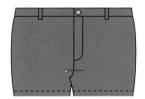

Figure 1

2. Measure and record width and length measurements:
Width—Measure the cut edge of the jeans. _____
Length—Holding jeans at your waistline, measure the length from the cut edge to the desired underskirt bottom edge, then add 1 inch. _____

3. Fold underskirt fabric in half lengthwise and then crosswise. Pin to hold in place. Tie a pencil to a string. Divide the width measurement by four, then add the length measurement. Mark the string this length from the pencil and, holding the mark at the tip of the fold, draw a curve. Cut on the curved line through all thicknesses, reserving cut-out circle. Staystitch ½ inch from cut edge, using a medium-long stitch.

4. Use cut-out circle as a pattern to cut out center of top skirt/scarf, matching centers (Figure 2). Staystitch ½ inch from cut edge of top skirt using a medium-long stitch. Finish cut edges of both skirts and jeans using serger or zigzag stitches.

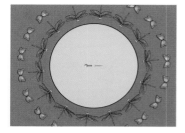

Figure 2

5. Mark center front and back of top skirt at cut edge, directly above top-skirt points. With right sides together, pin skirt to jeans, matching cut edges, and center fronts and backs. Sew, using a ⅝-inch seam allowance and easing or stretching to fit as needed.

6. Hem underskirt using a serged rolled hem or a narrow machine hem. Fold underskirt in half and mark center front and back. Pin to jeans over top skirt with right side facing previous stitching. Stitch using ⅝-inch seam allowance, checking that top skirt is not caught in stitching.

Figure 3   **Figure 4**

7. Hem edges of scarf center fabric with a serged rolled hem to make a rose. Hold at center and put a rubber band around fabric about midway (Figure 3). Turn edge fabric back over center and place a rubber band about halfway again (Figure 4). Turn it up and arrange fabric. ❖

Denim Delight

DESIGN BY LORINE MASON

A thrift-store jean jacket is given new life with fabric paints and the addition of elegant trims. Explore the artist within while creating one-of-a-kind wearable art.

FINISHED SIZE
Your size

MATERIALS
- Jean jacket
- 1 yard navy eyelash yarn
- 3 yards ½-inch-wide navy gimp trim
- Fabric paint:
      fuchsia
      blue
      light green
      white
      turquoise
      copper metallic
- 1-inch-wide foam brush
- Artist paintbrushes:
      Liner
      ¼-inch angle
- Masking tape
- Paper towels
- Basic sewing supplies and equipment

PROJECT NOTES
Use instructions as a guide only and adapt to suit your specific jacket design.

Mask off adjoining areas on jacket with masking tape before painting.

Apply two base coats, letting dry after each coat.

INSTRUCTIONS
1. Base-coat areas of jacket as follows using foam brush:
- Blue—front panels, side pocket openings and back yoke.
- Fuchsia—center back panel and front yokes.
- White—front pocket flaps.

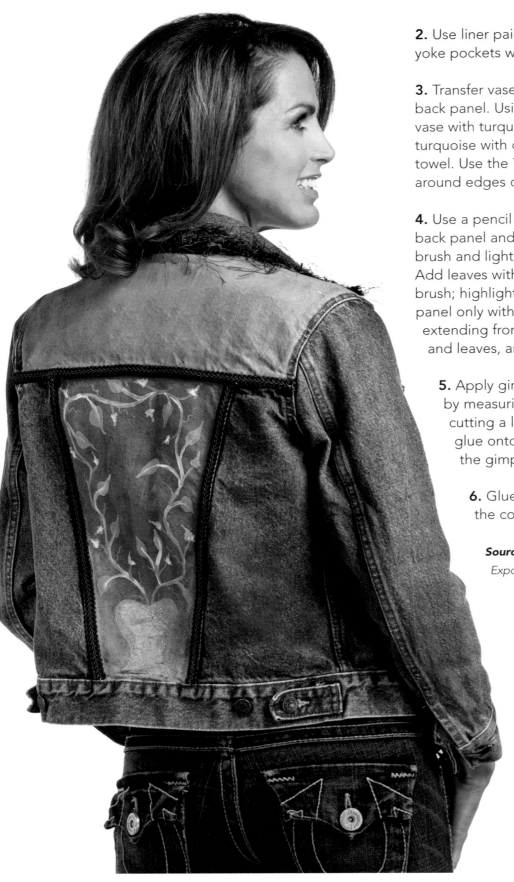

2. Use liner paintbrush to outline edges of front yoke pockets with fuchsia.

3. Transfer vase template onto bottom of center back panel. Using the foam brush, paint the vase with turquoise; let dry. Lightly sponge over turquoise with copper using a damp paper towel. Use the ¼-inch angle paintbrush to paint around edges of vase with copper; let dry.

4. Use a pencil to draw vines and stems on back panel and front yokes. Paint using liner brush and light green, highlighting with white. Add leaves with light green using the ¼-inch brush; highlight with white. Add flowers on back panel only with turquoise and white. Paint vines extending from pockets with light green vines and leaves, and fuchsia flowers.

5. Apply gimp trim to jacket fronts and back by measuring the area to be covered and cutting a length of trim. Generously spread glue onto the back of the trim, then press the gimp onto the jacket. Let dry.

6. Glue eyelash yarn around the edge of the collar in the same manner. ❖

Source: Gimp trim and eyelash yarn from Expo International.

TIPS & TECHNIQUES

Copy the design onto tear-away stabilizer using a pencil. Place the stabilizer on top of the denim. Use matching thread and sew over the design to transfer. Paint over the design to hide the stitching.

Vase

Denim Delight
Template
Actual Size

See, Shop, Sew

3M
(888) 364-3577
www.3m.com

BEACON ADHESIVES INC.
(914) 699-3405
www.beaconcreates.com

CLOTILDE
(800) 772-2891
www.clotilde.com

CREATIVE CRYSTALS CO.
(941) 331-4321
www.creativecrystal.com

DECOART
(800) 367-3047
www.decoart.com

EXPO INTERNATIONAL
(800) 542-4367
www.expointl.com

HANCY MFG. CO.
(866) 524-2188
www.fulllinestencil.com

LA FRED
(510) 893-6811
www.lafred.com

JONES TONES
(719) 948-0048, ext. 100
www.jonestones.com

PRYM CONSUMER USA INC.
www.prymdritz.com

SNAP SOURCE
(800) 725-4600
www.snapsource.com

SULKY OF AMERICA
(800) 874-4115
www.sulky.com

THERM O WEB
(800) 323-0799
www.thermoweb.com

TINY TREASURES FROM THE HEART
(941) 776-3737
www.tinytreasuresfromtheheart.com

THE WARM COMPANY
(425) 248-2424
www.warmcompany.com

Designers

Basic Sewing Supplies & Equipment

- Denim needle for sewing machine, ball point if using stretch fabric
- Hand-sewing needles and thimble
- Measuring tools
- Marking pens (either air- or water-soluble) or tailor's chalk
- Pattern tracing paper or cloth
- Point turners
- Pressing tools such as sleeve rolls and tailor's boards

- Pressing equipment, including ironing board and iron; press cloths
- Rotary cutter(s), mats and straightedges
- Sewing machine and matching thread
- Serger, if desired, with matching thread
- Scissors of various sizes, including pinking shears
- Straight pins and pin cushion

- Spray adhesive (temporary)
- Seam sealant
- Seam ripper